Original title:
The Attack of the Killer Snowballs

Copyright © 2024 Creative Arts Management OÜ
All rights reserved.

Author: Hugo Fitzgerald
ISBN HARDBACK: 978-9916-94-284-0
ISBN PAPERBACK: 978-9916-94-285-7

Glacial Grenades

In the park, the kids equip,
With snowballs stacked, the snowmen slip.
From behind the tree, they launch their round,
Giggles echo, chaos unbound.

A fluffy missile flies through the air,
Landing with a splat, without a care.
Round the corner, mom calls, 'Be polite!',
But snowballs fly, it's a snowy fight.

The Whiteout Whirlwind

Out in the storm, we leap and bound,
A flurry of fun, laughter resounds.
Snowflakes swirl, a frosty dance,
We plan our ambush, a wintery chance.

With madcap moves, we hit the ground,
Launching white missiles, joy unbound.
The snowman scouts, a snowy spy,
But watch out! Here comes a flying pie!

Winter's Wrath Unleashed

Cackling kids with snowballs dense,
They plot and scheme, it's quite intense.
With a slip and slide, the chase begins,
In this frosty game, no one wins.

We dodge and weave, a snowy spree,
Our laughter echoes, wild and free.
A snowball's flight, a comical sight,
Down goes a dad, oh what a fright!

Frosted Fury: The Snowball Siege

Armed with ammo, we take our stand,
Snowballs ready, the best in the land.
A quick launch here, and speedy retreat,
It's everybody's game, no one's discreet.

Amidst the chaos, a snowball flies,
And hits a friend with a gleam in their eyes.
The laughter erupts, as snowflakes collide,
In this wintry battle, we take it in stride.

Surprising Counterattack of Winter

Fluffy white soldiers drift from the sky,
Giggling children scoff, ready to comply.
They gather their ammo, a snowball brigade,
With laughter and cheers, their plans are laid.

Snowballs whiz past, a flurry of fun,
Chubby cheeks rosy, they scatter and run.
A cheeky snowman joins in the strife,
A snowball war burst, bursting with life!

But just when you think, they can't take more,
From behind a tree, a new troop will soar.
Furry squirrels armed with pinecones and glee,
Join the chaos, you better believe!

With every thrown snowball, the laughter grows wide,
Winters' slapstick antics, on this joyful ride.
Water drips down as the sunlight shines,
This snowy skirmish fills hearts with designs.

Ejaculations of Ice: A Snowy War

The air is thick, a chill of delight,
As frosty projectiles take off in flight.
Bouncing and squishing, the white fluff flies,
Squeaky giggles ring out, oh what a surprise!

Two teams collide, their laughter contagious,
Frosted cheeks shine, the mood is outrageous.
A target emerges, a friend on a sled,
With a perfect ice ball aimed right at their head!

A furry dog joins, he thinks it's a game,
Dancing through snow, he loves all the fame.
A snowball explodes, right in his face,
He barks with joy, oh what a wild chase!

The skirmish may end, but the joy won't cease,
With cheeks filled with snow and hearts filled with peace.

A wintery ruckus, where fun has its place,
As laughter echoes in this wintery space.

The Shimmering Chaos Unveiled

Winter's sparkle calls, come join the fun,
With snowflakes twirling, the thrill has begun.
Yonder lies chaos, in every white flake,
Gloves filled with projectiles, make no mistake!

The kids are a blur, with white fluff in tow,
Creating some mischief, making it glow.
A snowball flies by, takes out a poor hat,
The owner just laughs; he's constantly splat!

Old men in the park scowl with disdain,
Yet even they chuckle, they can't hide the gain.
Each toss brings giggles, no chance to be stern,
As we all join this riot, it's our turn to learn!

Winter's not just cold; it brings out the cheer,
An annual battle, full of love and no fear.
So grab a thick glove and join in the fray,
For every flurry holds joy, they say!

Playful Peril in the Winter's Realm

Fluffy flurries fall like feathers,
Creating chaos in the heather.
Laughter echoes in the air,
As snowballs soar with playful flair.

Bundled up like little bears,
They sneak and launch from secret lairs.
Giggles spill in snowy arcs,
As frosty mischief leaves its marks.

Run and duck, avoid the chill,
With each toss, some hearts could thrill.
The chill brings joy, pure and bright,
In this hilarious winter fight.

So guard your noggin, hold on tight,
The fluffy foes are in full flight.
With every throw, the world does gleam,
As we join in this frosty dream.

Shivering Soldiers of Snow

On the battlefield of white delight,
Snowmen stand, ready to take flight.
With carrot noses, they declare war,
On the kids who laugh and run for more.

Slick and icy, the ground beneath,
As frozen warriors hold their sheath.
In every toss, a giggling cheer,
Launching snowballs, never fear!

Helmeted hats and mittens on,
With each round, a new spawn drawn.
The battlefield, with snowmen strong,
Turns into a silly winter song.

Victory dances in the sun,
As everyone joins in on the fun.
The shivering soldiers laugh and play,
In this snowy game, bright as day.

Winter's White Reckoning

A blizzard brews with joy and glee,
Where snowballs fly, wild and free.
The frosty air is filled with shouts,
As laughter rolls, amidst the pout.

Children armed with frosty dreams,
Launch their shots with gleeful screams.
The chill ignites a playful dash,
While snowflakes fall with whimsical splash.

Each hit lands with a bubbly pop,
As giggles tumble, never stop.
The white-faced foes in playful trance,
Invite a merry snowball dance.

In this field of chilly cheer,
Encounters bold bring all near.
For in this freeze, the hearts will swell,
With joy that winter knows too well.

Frosty Fields of Fracas

In frosty fields where laughter reigns,
Snowballs fly like wild campaigns.
With mischief brewing in the cold,
Brave little souls are very bold.

Around the trees, with swift delight,
They plot their ambush, pure and bright.
A gleeful shout, the battle starts,
With snowy clumps, they race their hearts.

Chasing joy on icy trails,
Winter's chill behind their sails.
With every throw, a squeaky cheer,
As friendly fire finds its sphere.

Through frosty fields of merry fracas,
Each cheek aglow, a rosy focus.
In the end, when battles cease,
They share a laugh, and feel the peace.

Snowman's Revenge: Battle in the Blizzard

A snowman stood with bulging eyes,
His carrot nose aimed at the skies.
With an army of frosty friends in tow,
They plotted revenge on the kids below.

Cannonballs of snow with a fluffy surprise,
Launching from mounds, oh what a rise!
Snowballs flew from behind every tree,
As laughter erupted—what a sight to see!

The kids they squealed, dodges in place,
But the snowman grinned, ready for grace.
With chubby hands, they shaped and hurled,
In this winter battle, chaos unfurled.

At the end of the day, they all wound down,
With snowflakes dancing across the town.
A treaty was formed with a snowman's cheer,
And hot cocoa shared, spreading winter's cheer!

Frigid Fields of Fury

In frigid fields where frostbites land,
Snowmen gathered, making a stand.
With a sizzle of jingle bells on their heads,
They plotted mischief, while kids made their beds.

Whirls of white like cotton candy whirl,
Snowflakes falling, they began to twirl.
Chasing the children with laughter sounds,
Fury? Nah, just snowball rounds!

Soft, squishy balls with a dash of surprise,
Flew through the air like frigid pies.
Landing on cheeks with unbearable glee,
In this winter circus, everyone's free!

As twilight fell, they seized the day,
Chortles of joy in a snowy ballet.
The fields of fury turned fun once more,
In this winter tale, legends galore!

Bobbing Heads of Frost

In a winter wonderland, heads bobbing around,
Snowball fights started without a sound.
Frosty noggins with eyes so bright,
Began the adventure in pure delight.

White fluff flung in a merry chase,
Spinning and tumbling, each in their place.
Snowmen giggled with heads that swayed,
Frosted laughter—oh, how they played!

Caught in crossfire, a snowball flew!
Right at a snowman, it squeaked, 'Boo-hoo!'
But joy cracked through with each flurry tossed,
In this frosty battle, no one was lost.

As the evening wrapped this snowy spree,
The bobbing heads danced joyfully.
With hugs of snow and frosty cheer,
They vowed to return for another year!

Frosty Hands of Destruction

The frosty hands began to scheme,
Plotting their plans in a snowy dream.
With snowballs readied and giggles at hand,
The winter warriors made their stand.

Every toss sent laughter into the night,
With chilly treats flying left and right.
A flurry of fun, snow covered the ground,
With giggles and shrieks, joy knew no bounds.

In a war of fluff, together they roared,
Snowflakes falling, a victory scored.
But wait—what's this? A snowman's soft fate?
His head rolled off—oh, that's just great!

Yet even in chaos, they couldn't resist,
Crafting a snowman from tops to fist.
With frosty hands raised, they cheered once more,
In this whimsical battle, forever adored!

Fluffed Fury Unleashed

Round and soft, they roll around,
With laughter echoing through the ground.
A snowy horde prepared to fly,
With giggles rising to the sky.

They aimed with glee, no time to spare,
Launching fluff with crafty flair.
A slippery battle, all in sight,
As laughter mixed with frosty flight.

The frozen projectiles fly with pride,
While cheerful shouts are amplified.
Each toss a smile, a snowy kiss,
In this wintery, blissful bliss.

But watch your back, do take care!
'Cause snowballs lurk both near and far.
The fluffed fury, here to stay,
Turns every frown into a play!

White Fury: The Leisurely War

In the hush of snow, we gather pulse,
Ready, set, it's time to jolt!
Fluffy missiles, a soft attack,
With chilly humor, we won't hold back.

Outrageous laughter fills the air,
Snowflakes fly everywhere!
Laughter breaks, no one is shy,
Preparing for this wintry high.

Marshmallow fluff, all in the fray,
Batting snowballs, we dance and sway.
With grins as wide as winter's white,
The leisurely war is pure delight.

So gear up, friends, and take your stand,
With snowball ammo at your hand.
In cozy layers, we'll laugh and cheer,
As winter's antics draw us near!

Ice and Impulse: The Flake Fray

Snowflakes tumble, oh what a sight,
Inviting mischief, come join the fight!
With icy gloves and hearts aglow,
We charge the field, let chaos flow.

Aimed with laughter, quick on our feet,
Dodging and diving, what a treat!
Each fluffy orb, a joyous fling,
In this winter wonderland, we sing.

Who tossed that one? It's a mystery!
As snow falls down, around, so free.
With gleeful screams and playful thuds,
We'll fight till laughter is our flood.

So grab your gear, don't hesitate,
Join in the fun, we won't be late.
With ice and impulse, we won't be tamed,
This flake fray has us all proclaimed!

Whirling Snowflakes: A Tale of Winter Conflict

From rooftops high, they tumble down,
Creating chaos all around.
Whirling snowflakes take their aim,
The frosty skirmish turns to game.

With hearty giggles, we all engage,
In this swirling, snowy stage.
A flurry of laughter, bright and bold,
As winter tales of whimsy unfold.

We've got our gear, we're armed to play,
Each snowball launched, come what may!
With cheeks aglow and spirits bright,
A playful war brings pure delight.

So gather 'round, it's time for fun,
Let snowflakes dance 'til day is done.
In this tale of icy splendor,
Joy and laughter, we'll always remember!

Snowstorm Showdown

In the field we gather bright,
With snowballs packed, oh what a sight!
Laughter echoes as we prepare,
For a battle full of winter flair.

With icy arms we take our stand,
A fluffy fight, it's oh so grand!
Ducking and dodging, we do our best,
Snowflakes flying, it's all a jest.

Squeals of joy with every throw,
As fluffy rounds fly to and fro,
White projectiles dance in the air,
Who will win this chilly affair?

At last we drop, all worn out
In a pile of snow, we laugh and shout!
Victory unsure, but who will care?
Just friends and snow, a frosty fair.

Slippery Path to Glory

On the slope we bound with glee,
Where snowflakes swirl, wild and free.
A slippery path that leads us on,
With every slip, our grace is gone.

We tumble down, a snowball mess,
Rolling round, it's sheer excess.
In laughter's grip, we lose our way,
Chasing each other, come what may.

With chilly hands, we scoop and toss,
In this fierce fight, no one's the boss.
Snowballs soaring, some hit the mark,
Creating snow-splattered laughs in the park.

At last we stand, frozen in pride,
With cheeks aglow, no place to hide,
For in this fun, each throw brings glory,
A winter's tale, our fluffy story.

Hurling Flakes of Fury

With a waddle and a hop, we charge ahead,
Armed with snowballs, our cheeks all red.
"Take that!" we shout, with gleeful dismay,
As frosty grenades fly through the day.

Swiftly dodging, we twist and spin,
Each icy throw brings raucous din.
Our laughter echoes through the chill,
Every flake a thrill, oh what a skill!

Glorious chaos, our snowy brigade,
A field of warriors, in white arrayed.
We hurl with fervor, each one a star,
In this fluffy skirmish, we all go far.

As sunset beckons, we call it a night,
Friends bonded by laughter, a frosty delight.
In the aftermath, with snow in our hair,
A memory made, beyond compare.

Crystal Conflict

A frosty morn, the world shines bright,
With crystal glimmers, a pure delight.
We gather round, our hearts prepared,
For a playful showdown, all are scared.

Each snowflake glistens as they fall,
With gleeful giggles, we heed the call.
Swoop and dive, with all our might,
In this winter battle, we take flight.

Snowballs formed with a careful hand,
A fluffy fling, it's oh so grand!
Splats of laughter, all around,
In this sparkling war, joy is found.

At day's end, as shadows grow,
We count our hits, it's all in the show.
Friends united with snowy cheer,
A whimsical tale, we hold so dear.

Frosty Fury Unleashed

Snowballs sailing through the air,
Catching folks unaware!
Laughter echoes, oh what glee,
As winter's jesters dance with spree.

Frosty hats and scarves abound,
Snowy projectiles all around!
With each throw, a giggling fit,
In this frenzy, we won't quit!

Fluffy missiles zoom and glide,
Chasing friends, no place to hide.
A fluffy war, so full of cheer,
Winter's laughter, loud and clear!

Winter's Whimsical Assault

A snowball whizzes past my ear,
I duck and weave, but laugh, not fear.
Frosty fun on a sunny day,
In this battle, we laugh and play.

White fluff chaos fills the street,
As chilly projectiles we repeat.
With snowflakes flying far and wide,
A winter wonderland we can't hide!

Giggles burst like icy balls,
Laughter rings with cheerful calls.
This frosty fray is just the best,
In snowy antics, we find our rest!

Chilling Battlegrounds

The yard transformed, a snowy ground,
Where playful ruckus can be found.
I launch a flurry, hear the squeal,
In this freeze, it's all surreal!

Snowmen stand as silent guards,
While warriors toss their snowy shards.
With every squish, a happy sound,
In this chill, our joy is found!

A sudden strike, direct my way,
But I regroup and plan my play.
With laughter echoing in the air,
Our goofy war is beyond compare!

Hail of Icy Wrath

Here comes a volley, soft and white,
A frosty fight ignites tonight!
With rosy cheeks and hearts so bright,
We battle on in pure delight.

Snowflakes kiss our eager hands,
Creating chaos, making plans.
With every toss, a gleeful shout,
In this blizzard, there's no doubt!

Shenanigans ensue with joy,
Watch out now, oh dear boy!
As snowflakes swirl, we laugh and race,
In winter's grip, we find our place!

Chilling Assault of the Flurries

Upon the hill, they gather round,
A frosty troop without a sound.
They roll and pack, with giggles near,
Launching snowballs without fear.

A chilly blast, the battle starts,
Fluffy missiles, playful arts.
Who will win? Perhaps we'll see,
As flakes swirl in jubilee!

The laughter tallies with each throw,
Caught in the dance, our spirits glow.
For snow brings joy, with pure delight,
As winter's scene ignites the night.

In every corner, flakes unite,
Painting chaos in pure white.
A frosty fight, a funny spree—
The snowball fight's a sight to see!

Snowball Storm: A Frozen Fray

In fluffy drifts, we stake our claim,
A snowy war with no shame!
Armed with snow, we'll make our mark,
A flurry of fun ignites the park.

With laughter loud, we take our shot,
Dodging flurries from every spot.
The thrill of chase, as snowballs fly,
Oh what joy, beneath the sky!

We tumble down in winter's glee,
With snowflakes dancing merrily.
Each friendly hit met with a grin,
For in this chaos, we all win!

As daylight fades, our spirits rise,
A snowy fray, a sweet surprise.
Winter's charm, so full of cheer,
A playful fight we hold so dear!

Whispers of Ice and Chaos

A gentle breeze, a snowy hush,
In winter's game, we feel the rush.
Behind the trees, a plot unfolds,
The icy whispers, a tale retold.

Snowballs form with stealthy care,
A friendly siege is in the air.
With giggles soft, we plot our play,
Launching fluff in a mighty fray.

With every roll, the shouts emerge,
In snowy arcs, our laughter surge.
Each friendly hit sparks joy anew,
In winter's wild and funny view!

So let them fly, these frosty spheres,
We dance and dodge, dismiss our fears.
A flurry of fun on this bright day,
Where whispers of ice lead us astray!

Hail of White: A Snowy Ambush

A blanket white, the world ignites,
With friendly foes in snowy fights.
From behind the trees, we launch and cheer,
A playful storm is drawing near!

A flurry here, a flurry there,
With snowballs flying through the air.
Laughter echoes as we glide,
In this icy chaos, we'll confide!

The fluffy projectiles zooming fast,
With friendly faces unsurpassed.
Each snowball thrown, brings fits of giggles,
In this winter's dance, our joy just wiggles!

Though the temperature drops, our spirits soar,
A snowy ambush we all adore.
In every launch, in every dive,
Winter's fun keeps us alive!

Weeds of Ice and Snow

Fluffy foes in winter land,
Rolling round with snowball hand.
Not a weapon made of steel,
Just a pack of icy zeal.

Laughter echoes, watch them fly,
Hit your friend, oh my, oh my!
Sledding down with raucous joy,
Pelted good, but who's the boy?

Soft and white, they launch with glee,
Silly scenes for all to see.
Snowflakes scatter, giggles swell,
Who knew snow could cast such spells?

Even weeds in frozen ground,
Join the frolic, joy abound.
In the chill, we find our cheer,
Fighting snowball fun, oh dear!

The Snowdrift's Grudge

A mountain high, a drift of white,
Brimming with hopes to start a fight.
Snowballs ready, gathering might,
Which friend will face the frosty blight?

Behind the bushes, sneaky, sly,
Snowball ready, let it fly!
Laughter bursts, like frozen friends,
In this white wonder, fun transcends.

But wait, those drifts have had their say,
Rolling closer, no time to play.
Instead of dodge, it's time to run,
Chased by fluff, oh what fun!

The snowdrift plots its icy scheme,
Turning ordinary into dream.
With icy eyes, it glowers back,
In this fun, we lose our track!

Invasion of the Snow Combatants

From snowy peaks, they come in hordes,
Fluffy fighters with snowy swords.
Plundering smiles with every throw,
In this battle, friends are foes!

Behind the trees, they form their ranks,
Each snowball ready for the pranks.
A white barrage, the laughter roars,
Who knew winter had such scores?

Cover your head, that's the game,
A frosty clump, they'll stake their claim.
In this war, we lose all sense,
With every chuckle, we're on the fence!

The victor's crown, a hat of snow,
Funny tales that will surely grow.
Winter's magic plays its part,
Snow combatants win with heart!

Crystal Warfare: A Winter's Woe

In the field, the glimmers shine,
Crystal armies draw the line.
With frozen glee and icy flair,
Snowball tactics, beware, beware!

Launching fast, at every chance,
Who will dodge, who'll take a stance?
Laughter caught in flurries bright,
A winter dance, oh what a sight!

Exploding crystals all around,
Muffled giggles, no retreat found.
In this war of softest hits,
We're all in, without regrets!

Looks like winter's here to stay,
With frosty friends in joyous play.
From hidden nooks, the rebels shout,
Crystal battles, fun throughout!

Fluffy Brigade Strikes

In the glimmering white, a riot unfolds,
Snowballs are flying, daring and bold.
Giggling soldiers in marshmallow gear,
Launching their fluff with nothing to fear.

Behind snowy shields, they brace for the blast,
With laughter and squeals, they're having a blast.
Watch out for the flurries, they zoom through the air,
Hilarity reigns; it's a frosty affair.

Snowdrifts surround them, a treacherous land,
Yet giggles erupt as they all take a stand.
A fluffy brigade, with mischief in tow,
A warzone of ice, where joy starts to grow.

So grab your snowballs, let's join in the fun,
The fluffy brigade has only begun!
In this winter battle, where laughter won't cease,
Snowballing craziness brings moments of peace.

Snowbound Vengeance

With cheeks all aglow, they plot and they scheme,
Each snowball's a missile, each throw's like a dream.
The laughter erupts as they launch with a cheer,
A snowbound revenge, it's the highlight of the year.

From snow-covered roofs, the ambushes reign,
A wave of white madness, a comical strain.
They tumble and giggle, as snowballs ignite,
In this frosty blitz, everything feels right.

With friends by their side, they conquer the field,
Each volley of snow, their joy gets revealed.
Through snowflakes of chaos, their spirits collide,
In this whimsical battle, they take it in stride.

Snowbound vengeances, wrapped up in delight,
A flurry of laughter brings pure heartwarming light.
So let's join the fun in this silly refrain,
When snowballs are flying, there's nothing to gain.

Avalanche of Ice and Laughter

It starts with a chuckle, then snow starts to fly,
A sudden eruption, oh me, oh my!
A flurry of giggles, with ice in their hands,
The avalanche tumbles, creating new plans.

They dodge and they weave through the sparkling fluffs,
Tossing their ammo, they all call their buffs.
The battlefield's bright with a whimsical glow,
No peril today, just the laughter they sow.

Chasing through drifts, with snow to their knees,
Each snowball a treasure, each laugh brings them ease.
Their icy siege filled with vibrant delight,
An avalanche's charm on this bright winter night.

So join in the fun, feel the wintertime thrill,
With each throw of ice, they're climbing the hill.
An avalanche of laughter, where friendships are made,
In this world of snowflakes, let joy be displayed.

The Snowball War Chronicles

Once upon a time, in a world made of white,
The snowball wars raged, with all of their might.
With laughter as ammo, they strategize near,
Each round is a story, let's give them a cheer!

They gathered their forces, a troop full of glee,
On snowy horizons, they dreamed to be free.
With playful ambition, the snowballs were stacked,
In this animated tale, no joy is attacked.

As fairytale battles unfold in the frost,
They laugh and they tumble, no fun is ever lost.
In the chronicles told, let the stories unwind,
When snowballs are flying, hearts are aligned.

So gather your buddies, let's write this anew,
With laughter as ink, we'll paint winter's view.
A tale of pure joy, where cold meets a smile,
In the snowball war chronicles, we'll dance for a while.

Raging White Battalions

In the field, a snowy brigade,
Shaped like warriors, not afraid.
With laughter booming through the air,
They gather 'round without a care.

Marshmallow dreams, in fluffy rows,
Rolling hard, while winter blows.
Launching spheres with cheeky glee,
It's a fluffy war, as fun can be.

The snowmen cheer from by the trees,
As white balls soar on chilly breeze.
Giggles echo with each big splash,
Victory claimed with every crash.

Flurries of Fear: A Winter's Tale

Flakes of white come tumbling down,
Not a creature wears a frown.
Snowballs poised with crafty aim,
The frosty jesters win the game.

A snowball flies, the laughter swells,
Kings and queens of frosty spells.
Oops! A hit to mom's warm cheek,
"Now the fun's gone out of peak!"

Chasing tails in winter's dance,
All it takes is just one chance.
With squishy hits, the gleeful foes,
In this wonderland, anything goes.

The Great Snowball Uprising

Upon the hills, a battle starts,
Snowy spheres fly, pierce like darts.
Snowball warriors take their stand,
With frozen fists, they rule the land.

Tucked away in winter's nook,
A giant snowman took a look.
With icy grin, he called the troops,
Together forming snowy groups.

A flurry hit—oh what a sight!
Laughter reigns; the mood is bright.
The snowy army rolls and shouts,
For every throw, there's no doubts.

Icy Onslaught in Wonderland

In a land where snowflakes play,
Frigid jesters start their fray.
Snowballs seek their softest target,
A fluffy feast, a grand new market.

Carts of snow, and sleds abound,
Giggles echo all around.
With each fly-by, there's a cheer,
Watch the rosy faces near!

A frozen frenzy fills the air,
What chaos, what fun to share!
And with each laugh, the snowball flies,
As winter's spirit fills the skies.

Whirling White Menace

Chill winds blow, they start to form,
Round and fluffy, a snowy swarm.
Giggles rise from every street,
As snowballs tumble, oh what a feat!

A frosty face, a playful smirk,
Here they come, those icy quirks.
Dodge and weave, it's a blast,
Who knew winter could be so fast?

With each throw, our laughter rings,
Snow flies high, like snowy wings.
In the fray, our worries cease,
As we wage this frosty peace!

At the end, we lay in piles,
Covered in snow, we share our smiles.
With frosty joy, the day is done,
Who knew snow could bring such fun?

Frostbite and Flight

Snowflakes dancing in the air,
We chuck our ammo without care.
With laughter echoing all around,
Our icy war, in joy, we're bound!

Armor made of coats and hats,
The snowball fight ignites like chats.
Aiming high or low, we fling,
Each hit inspires a new zing!

A friendly hit, a mock dismay,
What fun we have throughout the fray!
Laughter rising as we retreat,
Nature's chill feels like a feat!

At last we're soaked, a snowy troop,
With frozen toes, we gather the scoop.
Time for hot cocoa, smile and cheer,
Our frosty war, a thing to revere!

Blizzard's Playful Siege

A sudden snowstorm, oh what joy!
Time to battle with every toy.
Snowballs tucked in jackets tight,
Ready for a frosty fight!

The snowflakes fall, we craft with glee,
Building forts, just wait and see!
We launch and laugh, what a delight,
In our blizzard, we take flight!

A well-aimed throw, a snowy splat,
You take that, and I'll have that!
Joyful shouts fill the white expanse,
In every ball, there lies a chance!

With frosty cheeks and hearts so bright,
The day wraps up with warm moonlight.
As snowmen stand, our triumph clear,
A snowy day we hold so dear!

Cold Confrontation

Noses red and cheeks aglow,
The time has come for winter's show.
Decked out in layers, we take a stance,
Prepared for mayhem, ready to dance!

Throwing snow while sipping tea,
Life's little battles full of glee.
With every toss, our laughter soars,
In this icy realm, friendship pours!

One hit's a miss, a comical fall,
Who would've thought that snowballs call?
In chilly bursts, we're caught in play,
Warming hearts in such a cold way!

At last we gather, tired but bold,
Sharing tales of the snowball gold.
With frosty minds, the fun won't cease,
In winter's realm, we find our peace!

When Snowflakes Turned Rogue

Once playful flakes that twirled and danced,
Now plotting schemes as if they had pranced.
Building their army, all fluffy and white,
They'd soon cause chaos, oh what a sight!

With giggles and laughter, they gathered in groups,
Forming a team of mischievous troops.
Snowmen were the captains, all ready for fun,
While snowballs were launched, oh, weren't they done?

A blizzard of giggles erupted around,
As fluffy projectiles zipped and spun 'round.
Every hit caused laughter, not shivers of fright,
Winter's wild children, a whimsical sight!

But as the sun glimmered and warmed up the day,
Those rascally snowballs all melted away.
Just puddles remained of their frosty brigade,
Yet memories lingered of the fun they had made!

Chill of the Frosty Fighters

Outside in the yard, the breath hangs in air,
Chilly little snowballs, with naught a care.
They gather together, plotting their throws,
In a flurry of laughter, their mischief just grows.

Children in jackets, bundled up tight,
As snowballs go flying, oh, what a sight!
Dodging and diving, ducking for cover,
The battle of giggles, they'll soon discover.

With puffs of white powder and faces aglow,
Winter's fateful warriors take to the snow.
Though frosty and fierce, it's all in good cheer,
The chill of their antics brings rapture, not fear.

By dusk, when the laughter begins to wane,
They find peace in snowflakes, there's no need for pain.
Frosty fighters retreat with hearts full of glee,
Until the next winter brings chapters anew, you see!

Ice-Encased Mayhem

What's this commotion? A shatter of peace,
When icy orbs launched, their flight won't cease.
A careful creation—a snow fort so grand,
Now under assault from a well-aimed hand!

Cackles and giggles fill all of the night,
As snowballs fly fast in the moon's silver light.
Each splat brings a chuckle, a gleeful delight,
In this frosty escapade, oh, what a sight!

The warmth of the homes calls them back with a cheer,
But the thrill of the chase keeps them huddled near.
With moans of defeat, the soft snow goes flying,
Ice-encased mayhem, it's silly, not dying!

When morning arrives, all chaos will fade,
But tonight is for laughter, not memories made.
For in each snowy fling, a story is spun,
Of seasons of fun, as they play, jump, and run!

A Flurry of Fists and Snow

In the glistening white, where mischief unfolds,
Groups of young faces with laughter so bold.
They chatter and squeal, making snowballs round,
In a frosty showdown, such joy to be found!

The flags are unfurled, let the battle begin!
With cheers and shrieks as they hurl with a grin.
Fists filled with snow, each throw like a race,
In this flurry of fun, there's no room for grace.

Some tumble and roll, some slip and they slide,
All covered in snow, they take it in stride.
With cheeks rosy red, and smiles oh-so wide,
The joy of the winter is hard to divide!

When the shadows grow long, in the fading of light,
The laughter still echoes in the cold of the night.
Each flurry of fists and snow holds its place,
In hearts full of joy, that forever will chase!

Winter's Soft Yet Steely Surrender

Fluffy white armies march with glee,
Each snowball crafted, a chilling decree.
Laughter erupts as cheeks start to glow,
Winter's soft charm puts on quite a show.

A barrage of giggles fills the cold air,
With snowflakes bouncing, oh what a dare!
In the playground, the battles commence,
Fortresses built, laughter's defense.

Mittens and hats tossed with zeal,
Each snowy encounter, a playful deal.
Chasing and dodging, with joy intertwined,
Winter's wild war, so sweetly designed.

As snowballs fly, it's pure delight,
With frosty laughter glimmering bright.
In this whimsical clash, all are friends,
Winter's embrace, where joy never ends.

Battle in the Flurries

In a flurry of white, the fun begins,
Snow drifts piled up, ready for spins.
With cheeks rosy red, and laughter in tow,
The fluffy skirmish is set to grow.

Sleds zooming by, a dash and a slide,
Snowballs whizzing, a wintery ride.
Whiffs of hot cocoa await for the brave,
In this chilled arena, friendships we save.

The ground shakes with laughter, the spirits soar,
Every splash of white prompts cries of encore.
Caught in the thrill of a snowball fight,
Joy dances freely in the pale twilight.

Amidst all the giggles and twinkling eyes,
Winter's pulling pranks beneath graying skies.
The snow may fall, but spirits won't freeze,
For laughter and joy bring the heart to ease.

The Chilling Challenge

A silent world cloaked in icy grace,
Snowball warriors ready to face.
With powdery globes and mittens so warm,
The chill in the air holds mischief's charm.

Targets marked out, it's game on today,
With squeals of delight in the playful fray.
Cold fingers soar as they launch and release,
Each throw a summons of giggles and peace.

Fluffy projectiles meet laughter's embrace,
In this winter wonder, there's no time to waste.
A parade of snowflakes, a flurry of cheer,
In the midst of the cold, friendship draws near.

With countable snowballs, mischief does bloom,
Who knew winter's chill would brighten the room?
Each snowball thrown is a memory made,
In the heart of the frost, joy will never fade.

Frozen Weapons of Joy

Armed with snowballs, so round and white,
Children prepare for a frosty delight.
The world is a canvas of playful strife,
In this icy arena, we find our life.

Tossing and dodging, we whirl and we spin,
Laughter erupts as we take it all in.
The snowflakes dance in the brisk winter air,
Each throw a reminder of joy that we share.

Face full of snow, yet laughter will reign,
In this frozen battleground, far from disdain.
The thrill of the chase, a budding romance,
In this chilly chaos, we gladly prance.

Cocoa awaits post the fun and the chill,
With marshmallows floating, warmth we will fill.
In icy embrace, we craft memories bright,
In the snowy playground, our spirits take flight.

Clash of the Cold: It's Snow Time!

Snowflakes gather, plotting with glee,
A fluffy brigade, wild and free.
They roll and tumble, form a big ball,
Ready to launch, they're having a ball.

With giggles and squeals, they gather in packs,
Chasing each other, dodging the flacks.
A snowman stands guard, but he won't last long,
When snowballs and laughter become the new song.

Each hit brings a smile, no one gets hurt,
As hats fly away, it's all in good sport.
The sun peeks through, and they all start to freeze,
But the joy in their hearts will never decrease.

In this winter wonder, let the fun unfold,
With chilly antics, as stories are told.
So pack up your snow, let's have some fun,
In this frosty battle, we're all number one!

Frozen Flanks: Battle in the Snow

The snowmen march, their buttons all bright,
With carrot noses, they're ready to fight.
Fleecy foes lining up for the show,
It's winter's laughter, let the games go!

With a whirl and a twirl, the battle begins,
As cold winds blow, they strategize wins.
Snowballs whizzing like comets through air,
The neighbors all watch with curious stare.

Then one cheeky flake rolls right down the slope,
Slipping and sliding, it's all downhill hope.
A barrage of giggles, the air thick with cheer,
As snowmen topple, the victory's near!

When plows clear the field and day turns to night,
The joy of the tussle will linger in sight.
Frozen flanks gather their scarves and hats tight,
Till the next snowy morn, when the fun will ignite!

The Crystal Conspiracy

A sparkly plot in the frosty blue light,
With mischief in mind, oh what a delight!
Tiny snowflakes whisper behind snowy walls,
Conspiring to launch the most fierce of snowballs.

With igloos as bases and snow forts as shields,
They strategize laughs on these snowy fields.
Snow-dogs in costume, ready to cheer,
While snow-soldiers chuckle, the enemy is near.

The leader, a snowman, with hat tipped askew,
Gives a wink to his team as the countdown renews.
One, two, three – let them fly with great glee,
While snowflakes fall soft, as happy as can be!

In this frosty tale without fear or dread,
The laughter of children is the vision ahead.
Let the world watch on in this spectacle bright,
As ice and pure joy dance under moonlight!

Frost-Kissed Combatants

In the frosty bright morn, the fun comes alive,
As snowballs are flung, oh how they thrive!
With frosty cheeks rosy, they dart to and fro,
Each hit is a victory in this playful show.

The chill in the air mixes with laughter and cheers,
As snowflakes clump tightly, assembling in spheres.
Little feet crunching on this winter's delight,
With snowmen on guard, ready for a fight.

A blizzard of giggles, oh what a mess,
As frost-kissed combatants give it their best.
The thrill of the chase on this white canvas spread,
In the heart of the battle, the fun lies ahead.

With the day growing old, their energy wanes,
But memories linger, like sweet little chains.
As the stars take their place and the sun hides away,
The laughter continues, in dreams they will play!

Deluge of Frozen Fun

A flurry comes from up the hill,
A snowy mass it's hard to spill.
With laughter ringing in the air,
We dodge and weave without a care.

The snowballs fly like tiny missiles,
As giggles follow each warm sizzle.
With frosty hands and cheeks aglow,
We battle like pros, oh what a show!

The world around is white and bright,
We're warriors in this frosty fight.
A snowball flies, but miss it does,
We cheer and shout because it was!

The playful hits are all in jest,
Friend against friend, we know the best.
A winter's day, pure joy to feel,
In snow-drenched fun, our laughter's real.

Icy Encounters and Sweeping Arrows

From rooftops high the snowflakes glide,
While sneaky hands hold one aside.
A perfect shape, the secret's there,
An icy arrow whizzes through the air.

With fluffy tomes and winter's cheer,
Warriors armed without a fear,
The snowballs kiss our fluffy hats,
We charge ahead, now who's the brat?

The laughter echoes down the lane,
With every throw, we feel no pain.
Our faces cold, yet hearts are bright,
In this snowy field, we find delight.

With cheeks aglow and spirits high,
We mount our steeds of snow and fly.
The icy battles never cease,
In frosted realms, we find our peace.

Arctic Anarchy

Unleashed they come, a frosty horde,
Each warrior poised, with snowball stored.
A night of chaos, fun takes flight,
In winter's grasp, we own the night.

With shouts of joy and giggles loud,
Our snowball fight, it's fun, we're proud.
The world is cold but warm within,
For every loss, there's still the win!

Round and round, we chase and break,
The laughter rings, a jolly quake.
Walls of snow, ten feet so high,
We scale them fast, oh my, oh my!

In this wild dance of pure delight,
We're kings and queens of snowy night.
So let them fly, let spirits soar,
In chilly glee, we all want more!

White Out Warfare

In fluffy ranks, the snowmen stand,
Preparing for a battle grand.
Each soft-packed ball, a creature born,
In hectic fun, we are reborn.

Watch out the door, it's danger sweet,
With perfect aim I can't be beat!
Each round designed with crafty care,
In this winter's dream, we're unaware.

We roll and tumble with glee and mirth,
In frosty fields of playful earth.
The chilly air, a kiss so pure,
A fleeting moment we'll endure.

As snowflakes fall like whispered sighs,
The joy of winter never dies.
In battles fought with laughter bright,
We live our dreams 'til comes the night.

Frosty Skirmish in the Park

In the park where giggles spring,
Snowballs soar like birds on wing.
Little hands work fast and fleet,
Laughter echoes, a merry beat.

Gloves are soggy, cheeks are pink,
Snowmen wobble, heads in sync.
A frosty wind, a playful hiss,
Who knew snow could bring such bliss?

Unexpected ambush from behind,
Sister's laughter is unconfined.
Payload lands, a friendly throw,
In this battle, all's for show.

As the day winds and shadows grow,
Snowball remnants, a fluffly glow.
Frosty fun, a fleeting glee,
Winter's joy, wild and free.

Winter's Hidden War

Beneath the trees, a strategy forms,
Snowballs mold in various norms.
Sly faces peek from burrows near,
A plan unfolds, excitement clear.

Snowflakes gather, tails a-flare,
Giggles rise from chilled young air.
Loyal troops in jackets bright,
Ready to launch with all their might.

A sudden strike, oh, what a sight,
Snowball showers take to flight.
Cheery yells and playful screams,
Winter wonder, snowfall dreams.

But with a slip, a surprise attack,
Down they tumble, laughter's knack.
Covered in snow, they cheer so loud,
Winter's war, a festive crowd.

A Snowy Ruckus at Dusk

As dusk descends, the battle brews,
Snowballs formed in vibrant hues.
Sneaky eyes and smirking grins,
The frosty fun about begins.

Warming hands in chilly air,
Swooping low with skillful flair.
A sneaky throw, a icy plot,
Caught off guard, oh, what a shot!

Shouts of glee fill the evening sky,
Snowflakes whirl, oh my, oh my!
A flurry here, a splatter there,
Joyful pandemonium everywhere.

As the light fades, the fun remains,
Covered in snow, hearts have no chains.
Tomorrow's sun will melt away,
But winter's laughter here will stay.

The Iceborne Revolt

From the rooftops, the snowflakes gleam,
Children plot, with laughter's scheme.
A rebel roar, a snowy cheer,
It's a snowy day, let's persevere!

Battle lines drawn in the white,
Siblings armed, ready to fight.
A snowy fortress built with glee,
Each fluffy round as soft as can be.

The first fling, a direct hit,
Furry jackets, they won't quit.
Snowflakes dance in joyful flight,
A winter skirmish, pure delight.

With a powdery puff and a merry sound,
The king of snowballs is finally crowned.
Amid the laughter, the fun ignites,
In this frozen world, all feels right.

Snowflakes Turned Soldiers

Tiny soldiers on the ground,
Ready to leap, without a sound.
They twirl and dance, a frosty ball,
In winter's grip, they heed the call.

With laughter ringing through the air,
These flurries plot without a care.
A toss, a toss, they find their aim,
In a snowball fight, it's all a game!

The lucky ones with powdery hats,
Join their friends and play like brats.
Snowmen cheer, they want in too,
On this frosty hullabaloo!

But watch your back, oh snowy foe,
For flakes can pack a mighty throw.
In this blizzard of fun, oh what a thrill,
These tiny soldiers come for the kill!

Frostbite's Daring Duel

In a winter wonderland so bright,
Frostbite's mischief takes to flight.
Snowball warriors march with glee,
Plotting fun for you and me!

A duel begins, the air is filled,
With laughter loud, no hearts are chilled.
Each throw a giggle, each splash a cheer,
In this frosty battle, there's nothing to fear!

Warm gloves ready, they charge ahead,
With icy projectiles, they will shred.
The sun may shine, but watch your toes,
For danger lurks where the cold wind blows!

When winter calls, let's take a chance,
Join the snowflakes in a playful dance.
A frosty truce when the day is done,
But oh, that duel was oh-so-fun!

Avalanche of the Playful

Here comes an avalanche, full of cheer,
A wave of snowballs, drawing near!
Children giggle, the air is bright,
Ready for laughter, an epic fight!

With every throw, a silly squeal,
Frosty warriors spinning like a wheel.
Green hats, red mittens, all in a race,
No time to pout, there's fun to chase!

Watch out, my friend, for a snowy sneak,
A flurry strikes, and it's laughter they seek.
They bounce and roll in this snowy spree,
This avalanche brings joy, oh can't you see?

As the sun sets, the papers lie,
In cozy piles where snowballs fly.
They gather 'round, our snowy crew,
An avalanche of joy for me and you!

Crystal Combat in the Snow

In a land of frost with spirits high,
Snowflakes twinkle, oh me, oh my!
A snowy battle in the crisp white glow,
Where crystal combat starts to flow!

With cheeky smiles and chilly shouts,
The snowball bounces, laughter sprouts.
Foes become friends, in this icy spree,
Creating memories for you and me!

Snow forts built with crafty hands,
Defend our turf, make your stands!
A fierce exchange, they tumble and roll,
As joy ignites in every soul!

When dark clouds gather and night descends,
We gather closer, all are friends.
With stories shared of this snowy play,
Crystal combat brightens our day!

Winter's Whimsy Turns Wicked

A snowman grinned with a frosty sneer,
As flurries flew in a wild cheer.
They circled close, a mischievous horde,
With icy eyes, they raised their sword.

Laughter rang as the pellets flew,
Chattering teeth, a frosty zoo.
They wrapped up tight in their puffy gear,
But winter's game was far from clear.

Snowballs bounced with a playful thud,
In this chill, giggles turned to mud.
Watch where you step, watch where you play,
For winter's fun might just stray!

In a flurry of white, chaos reigned,
As snowballs danced like they were trained.
Frosty mischief in every throw,
Who knew the snow could be so woe?

Icy Chances in the Air

With sudden flair, the snowflakes spun,
Underfoot, they sizzled, oh what fun!
A plushy pelt of white delight,
Unleashed a storm, a snowy fight.

Armed with laughter and chill-filled shouts,
Kids formed crews, while fearsome doubts,
Of icy doom danced through the night,
Each launch a chance—what a funny sight!

Snowballs whizzed like missiles bright,
Targeted your buddy—what a sight!
Laughter echoed, the fun arose,
With every hit, a new tale grows.

A flurry of giggles, a whiff of cold,
In this winter tale of lives retold.
With every throw an icy blast,
A charming chaos, we'll hold it fast!

Frosty Rebellion: The Snow's Revenge

A fluffy foe with eyes so sly,
Conspired to blanket the earth awry.
Snowballs armed like tiny grenades,
With giggling troops, their joy cascades.

In yards they gathered, a frosty force,
With mighty aims, they'd chart their course.
No one was safe from the icy rain,
As laughter burst, and humor gained.

A whirling blizzard of giggles flew,
As snow smashed gently against you too.
With cheeks aglow and bellies ache,
They plotted pranks with every flake.

For these frosty rebels danced in glee,
In a winter war, so wild and free.
With every hit, a story shared,
A frosty tale, by all declared!

Luminescent Battles of Ice

Glowing white against the night,
Snowballs rolled, a comical fight.
The air buzzed bright with frosty cheer,
As warriors gathered, nothing to fear.

With giggles loud, they formed a line,
In winter's glow, all felt divine.
Each snowball tossed, a glittering arc,
Light danced and flickered, a snowy spark.

Cheeks rosy, laughter ringing clear,
They launched their rounds with festive cheer.
In this luminous fight, joy took flight,
As friends became foes, in pure delight.

A battle of whimsy in the moonlit air,
With snowflakes swirling, no time to spare.
In frozen chaos, warmth would bloom,
Under the chill, laughter consumed!

Frozen Furies: Battle Unleashed

In the frost, the snowballs fly,
Laughter echoes, oh my, oh my!
Chasing friends down icy lanes,
Squeals of joy mixed with chills and pains.

Dressed in white, they launch their fire,
With every throw, their hopes aspire.
Laughter bursts as they collide,
In this winter, joy can't hide!

Snow forts built with all their might,
Prepare for war, it's pure delight!
With cheeks all red and spirits high,
A winter's tale that won't run dry.

Now retreat, the sun draws near,
But memories of fun stay clear.
Tomorrow's snow will call again,
For frozen furies to defend!

Snowball Warriors: A Cold Conquest

Armored up in layers thick,
Snowball fights, a sneaky trick.
Launching rounds with stealthy aim,
Victory sweet, a playful game.

Behind the mounds, they plot away,
Strategizing through the fray.
Giggles burst like snowflakes bright,
As they charge into the fight!

Whispers soft, then sudden blitz,
Ballooning laughter, what a mix!
Snowplows running near the road,
While we're caught, in winter's code.

At dusk, the battlefield grows still,
Exhausted from all the thrill.
In whispers soft, the legends grow,
Of snowball warriors, in winter's glow.

Flakes of Fury Falling Fast

Fluffy flakes fill up the air,
Winter's weapon, beyond compare.
With smirks they load their icy packs,
Ready for fun, no time to relax!

Each throw a joy, each dodge a cheer,
Roars of laughter grasping near.
Snowflakes swirl with a playful dance,
While everyone takes a snowy chance.

The cold bites, but hearts are warm,
United by this snowy charm.
With every hit, giggles take flight,
In this chaos, spirits ignite!

Now as the sun beams down so bold,
Stories of snowball wars are told.
As winter fades, they hold it dear,
The flakes of fury, a frosty cheer!

Snow's Surprising Assault

A white surprise falls from the sky,
Snow's warm welcome, oh my, oh my!
Armed with laughter, ready to go,
Snow's surprising fun steals the show.

Bundle up, here comes the chase,
A sudden snowball finds its place.
Unexpected splats and roars of glee,
Each round a sprinkle of jubilee.

Cheap thrills wrapped in frosty mist,
Making snowflakes dance and twist.
With cheeks all rosy, eyes aglow,
In this silly war, they steal the show!

As twilight sets on snowy ground,
Echoes of laughter still resound.
Fortresses made, glee never to cease,
Snow's surprise brings endless peace!

Snowy Skirmishes

A winter day, so bright and clear,
Children laugh, with nothing to fear.
Snowballs flying, a fluffy delight,
A snowy battle in sheer delight.

With puffs of white, they launch with glee,
Who will win? Just wait and see!
Giggles echo in the frosty air,
As snowballs soar with a playful flair.

The dog joins in, a furry blitz,
Chasing snowballs, his tail does flips.
But oh no, one flies just too high,
Hits Dad right in the eye!

The snowman stands, a judge so grand,
Watch the chaos as they make their stand.
With every toss, the fun is clear,
Snowy skirmishes bring lots of cheer!

Frosty Projectiles Fly

Gather 'round, kids, the snow is fresh,
Time to create a snowy mesh.
With frosty projectiles in our hands,
Here come the fun, in snowy lands!

The forts are built, in vibrant white,
Ready for battle, it's pure delight.
Aim for the targets, don't you dare miss,
A snowball fight feels like pure bliss!

The cat just watches, with wide-eyed stare,
As snowballs soar through the crisp cold air.
Laughter echoes, what a wild show,
Frosty projectiles, oh, how they go!

The sun starts setting, the day's nearing end,
But not before one last throw, my friend!
As snowballs fly and spirits soar,
We'll do it again, who could ask for more?

Winter's Frozen Fury

The wind howls, but we don't care,
In our winter gear, we run with flair.
Snowballs ready, we gear up tight,
   Winter's frozen anger ignites!

A flurry of snow, a blend of fun,
Watch as we dance, our battles begun.
With fluffy grenades, we laugh and shout,
   Winter's frozen fury, there's no doubt!

Tommy slips, but he's quick to rise,
Snow down his back, much to his surprise.
Yet with a grin, he throws one back,
   Our laughter rolls, no moment lacks!

A snowy avalanche, chaos prevails,
Amidst the laughter, we dodge the gales.
Though winter's mad, we take it in stride,
   Frozen fury, it's a joyful ride!

Cold Chaos Unfolds

Snowflakes flutter, calm before fight,
We prepare for a wild snowy night.
In our hearts, mischief takes hold,
As cold chaos unfolds, behold!

Aiming low, we plot our scheme,
Frosty dreams like a sparkling dream.
Snowmen stand, but they're not our foes,
All in good fun, as laughter flows!

With each chuckle, our team grows bold,
In this winter wonderland, shivers unfold.
Sledges and laughter, a sight to behold,
In this frosty fun, our joy is gold!

The sun sets low on this icy spree,
But we won't stop, we're wild and free.
For in the chill, we've made our marks,
Cold chaos travels, igniting sparks!

The Playful Snowmen's Revenge

In the yard they stand so round,
With knitted caps, a joy profound.
Snowflakes swirl, they plot and plan,
To toss those balls with icy span.

With cheeky grins, they take their aim,
With chilly glee, they play their game.
Snowballs fly with laughter loud,
Their snowy prank, a frosty crowd.

They dance and twirl, their movement swift,
A winter's joke, a chilly gift.
Giggles echo through the air,
Those snowmen's tricks, a frosty dare.

So beware, you soft and warm,
They'll cover you in icy charm.
With every throw, they've made it clear,
The playful snowmen have no fear!

Hurling Blizzard: A Brawl Unfolds

Amidst the clouds, the snow did roar,
A blizzard battle, and so much more.
From backyard forts, the kids all cheer,
As snowballs fly, winter's frontier.

Wielding snow, they dance and dive,
Each fluffy projectile helps them thrive.
With squeals of joy, they make a stand,
A snowy fight, so grand and planned.

With every hit, the laughter grows,
In giggle fits, the chaos flows.
A flurry of fun, with shouts and screams,
This snowy brawl fulfills their dreams.

So grab your gear, protection's wise,
Join in the fun, beneath grey skies.
With frosty ammo, you'll feel alive,
In this wintry war, we all will thrive!

A Dance of Snow and Danger

The ground is white, a sight so bright,
Beneath the moon, on this frosty night.
Snowflakes twirl like dancers bold,
In this wild tale, let's be told.

With a whoosh and a laugh, they start to play,
Rolling snowballs, hip-hip-hooray!
Through the frosty air, they soar and swoop,
A chilly ballet, a merry troupe.

They spin and leap, with glee uncontained,
The laughter echoes, the cold, unfeigned.
A faux pas here, a slip and slide,
In this dance of mirth, joy won't hide.

So twirl with me, don't be afraid,
In this fluffy waltz, good times are made.
With snow as our stage, let's take a chance,
In this playful scene, we'll dance and prance!

Snowball Blitz: A Merry Mayhem

In the moonlit night, they gather round,
With tiny hands, they make their mound.
Snowballs stacked up, oh what a sight,
The mischievous kids are ready to fight!

The first one flies, with a whistle and roll,
A snowball blitz, it's out of control!
With laughter ringing, the chaos reigns,
As frosty orbs collide, like playful trains.

Snowmen wobble as they join the fray,
More balls are thrown, they cheer and sway.
The landscape white, like a winter's dream,
This merry mayhem is a joyful theme.

Snowy glee fills the frosty air,
With every throw, you're free of despair.
So join the fun, grab your snowy stock,
In this winter wonder, let's all unlock!

Frosty Tactics on the Playground

In the glow of winter's light,
Kids armed with white delight,
Snowballs flying through the air,
Giggles echo everywhere.

Ducking low and taking aim,
Every child is in the game,
Laughter mixes with the chill,
Chasing down the snowy thrill.

Aiming for the perfect throw,
Hit your friends, just like in snow,
But watch out for a counterstrike,
As laughter turns into a hike.

When the sun begins to fade,
Snowball plans start to invade,
The fun will never truly stop,
Until the last snowball drops!

The Silver Brigade of Snow

Gathered in the frosty park,
Children launch a snowy lark,
Frosty balls of laughter fly,
As snowflakes dance from the sky.

Dressed in coats of vibrant hue,
The silver brigade's coming through,
With helmets made of braided ice,
Every toss a cool paradise.

They strategize with secret glee,
Snowmen stand in awe to see,
A winter wonderland ballet,
As snowballs bounce and children play.

But oh! A rogue ball finds its mark,
A giggle springs from out the dark,
The battle rages, joy ignites,
In snowy lands, pure delight!

Juggernaut of the Winter Storm

Amidst the flurries, kids will scheme,
Crafting snow into a dream,
The juggernaut rolls around,
With laughter as its playful sound.

Wielding weapons of the white,
Snowballs soaring, pure delight,
With every throw, a battle cry,
Winter warriors reach for the sky.

Uncontrolled chaos, see them glide,
In the frenzy, they collide,
A snowy dance of pure chuckles,
Joyful cries as winter struggles.

But as the day winds down to night,
Warm hearts bask in winter's light,
Swapping tales of snowy plight,
And laughing till the stars are bright!

An Icy Clash of Titans

A chilly breeze announces war,
Allies gather at the door,
The icy clash of focused aim,
In this battle, fun's the game.

Launching snowballs, quick and slick,
Dodging low with every trick,
Titan children gleefully shout,
As all their worries fade from doubt.

Mighty throws and joyful cheer,
Winter's spirit brings us near,
No one's safe from frosty fling,
Every child a snowy king.

As dusk descends with snowy grace,
We share warm drinks in this space,
Laughing tales of snowy brawls,
Echo in the frosty halls!

Milton Keynes UK
Ingram Content Group UK Ltd.
UKHW021951151124
451186UK00007B/184